Pebble® Plus

Presidential Biographies

John F. Kennedy

by Erin Edison

Consulting Editor: Gail Saunders-Smith, PhD

Consultant:
Sheila Blackford
Librarian, Scripps Library
Managing Editor, American President
Miller Center, University of Virginia

CAPSTONE PRESS
a capstone imprint

Pebble Plus is published by Capstone Press,
1710 Roe Crest Drive, North Mankato, Minnesota 56003.
www.capstonepub.com

Library of Congress Cataloging-in-Publication Data
Edison, Erin.
John F Kennedy / by Erin Edison.
pages cm.—(Pebble plus. Presidential biographies)
Includes bibliographical references and index.
Summary: "Simple text and full-color photographs describe the life of John F. Kennedy."—Provided by publisher.
ISBN 978-1-4296-8738-6 (library binding)
ISBN 978-1-62065-320-3 (ebook PDF)
1. Kennedy, John F (John Fitzgerald), 1917–1963—Juvenile literature. 2. Presidents—United States—Biography—
Juvenile literature. I. Title.
E842.Z9E35 2013
973.922092—dc23
[B]
                                                                2011049862

Editorial Credits
Erika L. Shores, editor; Sarah Bennett, designer; Wanda Winch, media researcher; Kathy McColley,
production specialist

Photo Credits
Corbis: Bettmann, 1, 19, The John F Kennedy Presidential Library and Museum, Boston: 7, 9, 11, Cecil Stoughton/
White House, cover, 21, Richard Sears, 5, Tony Frissel, 13; Library of Congress: Prints and Photographs Division, 15, 17

Note to Parents and Teachers

The Presidential Biographies series supports national history standards related to people and culture. This book describes and illustrates the life of John F. Kennedy. The images support early readers in understanding the text. The repetition of words and phrases helps early readers learn new words. This book also introduces early readers to subject-specific vocabulary words, which are defined in the Glossary section. Early readers may need assistance to read some words and to use the Table of Contents, Glossary, Read More, Internet Sites, and Index sections of the book.

Printed in the United States of America in North Mankato, Minnesota.
052013   007340R

Table of Contents

Early Years

John Fitzgerald Kennedy had big ideas for the United States. The future president was born in Massachusetts on May 29, 1917. He had eight brothers and sisters. His family and friends called him Jack.

1917

born in Brookline, Massachusetts

John F. Kennedy (left, back row) and his family in 1931

John's family was rich.

They sent him to the best schools.

John sometimes struggled
in school. He was often sick.

In 1940 he graduated from
Harvard University.

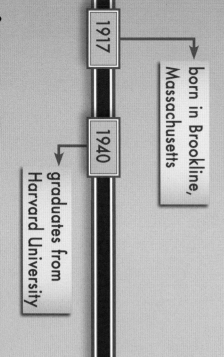

1917 — born in Brookline, Massachusetts

1940 — graduates from Harvard University

Young Adult

John joined the U.S. Navy in 1941.

Soon the United States entered

World War II (1939–1945).

John was the leader of a U.S. Navy

boat. When the boat sank, John

saved the lives of some crew members.

People called him a hero.

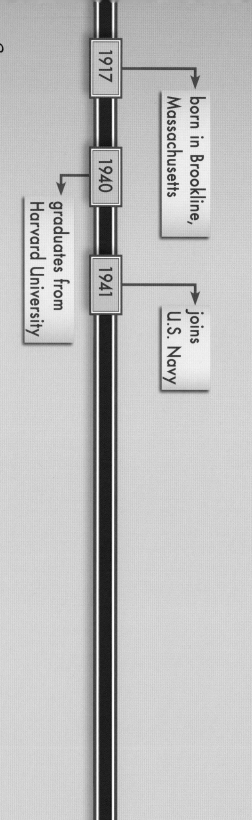

1917 — born in Brookline, Massachusetts

1940 — graduates from Harvard University

1941 — joins U.S. Navy

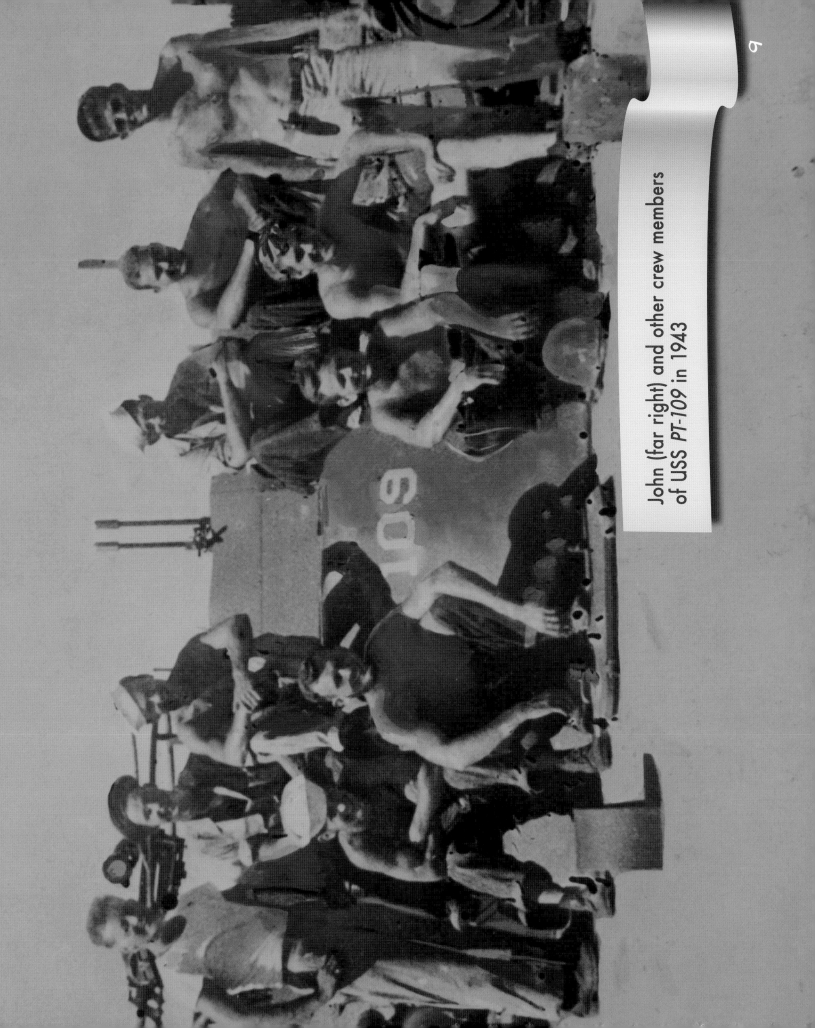

John (far right) and other crew members of USS *PT-109* in 1943

Starting in 1946, John was elected
to the U.S. Congress five times.
In 1956 John wrote *Profiles
in Courage.* In this book,
John wrote about leaders
and their ideas.

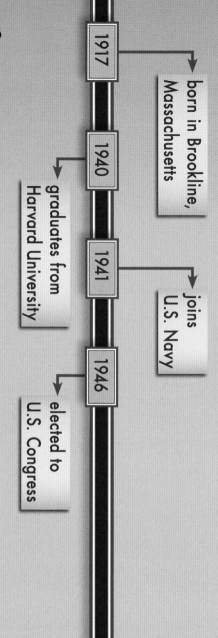

1917 — born in Brookline, Massachusetts

1940 — graduates from Harvard University

1941 — joins U.S. Navy

1946 — elected to U.S. Congress

John met Jacqueline Bouvier in 1951. Jacqueline, known as Jackie, was a photographer. John and Jackie married in 1953. Their daughter, Caroline, was born in 1957. John Jr. was born in 1960. Another son, Patrick, died soon after birth.

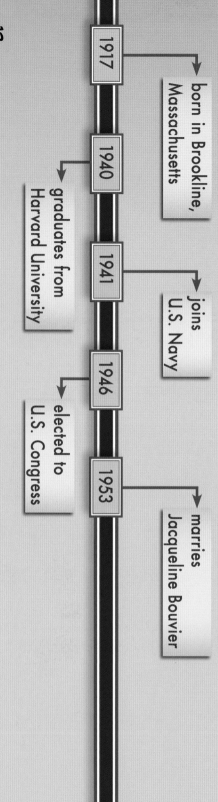

1917 — born in Brookline, Massachusetts

1940 — graduates from Harvard University

1941 — joins U.S. Navy

1946 — elected to U.S. Congress

1953 — marries Jacqueline Bouvier

President Kennedy

In 1960 John was elected the 35th president of the United States.

At age 43, he was the youngest man to be elected president.

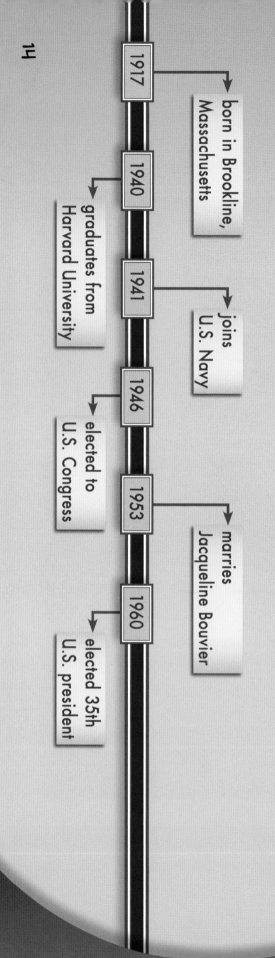

1917 — born in Brookline, Massachusetts

1940 — graduates from Harvard University

1941 — joins U.S. Navy

1946 — elected to U.S. Congress

1953 — marries Jacqueline Bouvier

1960 — elected 35th U.S. president

John's inaugural address on January 20, 1961

John was a busy president.

He worked for equal rights

and started the Peace Corps.

He also wanted Americans

to explore outer space.

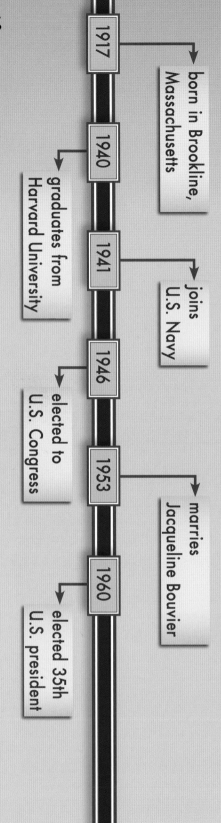

1917 — born in Brookline, Massachusetts

1940 — graduates from Harvard University

1941 — joins U.S. Navy

1946 — elected to U.S. Congress

1953 — marries Jacqueline Bouvier

1960 — elected 35th U.S. president

On November 22, 1963,

John and Jackie were riding

in a parade in Dallas, Texas.

John was shot and killed.

At just 46, he was

the youngest president

to die in office.

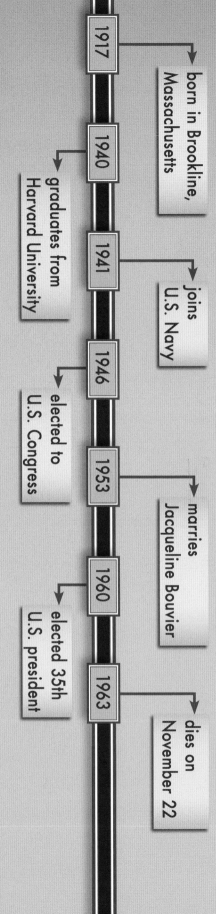

1917 — born in Brookline, Massachusetts

1940 — graduates from Harvard University

1941 — joins U.S. Navy

1946 — elected to U.S. Congress

1953 — marries Jacqueline Bouvier

1960 — elected 35th U.S. president

1963 — dies on November 22

Caroline, Jackie, and John Jr. at John's funeral on November 25, 1963

Remembering Kennedy

John was president for less than three years. But in that short time, he left a lasting mark on the country. People remember John F. Kennedy as a great leader.

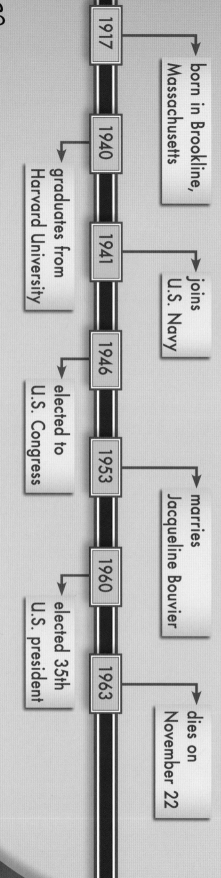

1917 — born in Brookline, Massachusetts

1940 — graduates from Harvard University

1941 — joins U.S. Navy

1946 — elected to U.S. Congress

1953 — marries Jacqueline Bouvier

1960 — elected 35th U.S. president

1963 — dies on November 22

Glossary

Congress—the elected government body of the United States that makes laws; Congress includes the Senate and the House of Representatives

elect—to choose someone as a leader by voting

equal rights—the things that laws allow all people to do, such as the right to vote or the right to speak freely, regardless of race or gender

graduate—to finish all the required classes at a school

Peace Corps—an organization of trained volunteers from the United States that helps people in other countries; Peace Corps volunteers often help people with farming and education

World War II—a war in which the United States, France, Great Britain, the Soviet Union and other countries defeated Germany, Italy, and Japan; World War II lasted from 1939 to 1945

Read More

Brown, Jonatha A. *John F. Kennedy. People We Should Know.* Milwaukee: Weekly Reader Early Learning Library, 2006.

Raatma, Lucia. *Jacqueline Kennedy. First Ladies.* Mankato, Minn.: Capstone Press, 2011.

Todd, Anne. *John F. Kennedy: A Life of Citizenship. People of Character.* Minneapolis: Bellwether Media, 2008.

Internet Sites

FactHound offers a safe, fun way to find Internet sites related to this book. All of the sites on FactHound have been researched by our staff.

Here's all you do:

Visit *www.facthound.com*

Type in this code: 9781429687386

Check out projects, games and lots more at
www.capstonekids.com

Index

Word Count: 281
Grade: 1
Early-Intervention Level: 23